Beloved Alcoholic

BELOVED ALCOHOLIC

What to Do When a Family Member Drinks

Janet Ohlemacher

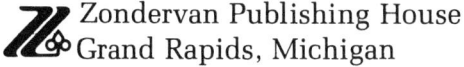
Zondervan Publishing House
Grand Rapids, Michigan

Zondervan Books are published by
Zondervan Publishing House
1415 Lake Drive, S.E.
Grand Rapids, Michigan 49506

BELOVED ALCOHOLIC
Copyright © 1984 by The Zondervan Corporation
Grand Rapids, Michigan

Library of Congress Cataloging in Publication Data
Ohlemacher, Janet.
    Beloved alcoholic.
    Bibliography: p.
    1. Alcoholics–Family relationships–Case studies. 2. Alcoholics–Rehabilitation–Case studies. 3. Alcoholism–Religious aspects–Case studies.
I. Title.
HV5132.047   1984   362.8'2   84-13114
ISBN 0-310-45531-6

All rights reserved. No part of this publication may be reproduced, stored in a retrieval system, or transmitted in any form or by any means without the prior permission of the publisher.

Edited by Julie Ackerman Link
Designed by Kim Koning

Printed in the United States of America

84 85 86 87 88 89 / 10 9 8 7 6 5 4 3 2 1

Contents

    Introduction   6
1. The Alcoholic Family   14
2. God Reaches Down   19
3. Plunging Backward   26
4. Moving Out in Faith   33
5. Programs Designed to Help   40
6. Intervention   48
7. Confrontation   58
8. Clout   67
9. Discovering Why We Failed   73
10. Legal Commitment   80
11. What's Left to Say?   87
    Epilogue   93
    Notes   95

Introduction

Today I did something I never thought I'd have the strength or courage to do. I signed the papers necessary to commit my mother to treatment—treatment she has steadfastly refused to seek for herself. Fifteen agonizing years brought me to this point, and I pray that I will never have to face such a decision again.

You see, my mother is an alcoholic. She not only drinks, she cannot control her desire for alcohol. Her drinking has caused her to sever relationships with family and friends, to suffer several serious falls, and to lose her job.

During these last four years, she has become a broken and lonely old woman. She is slowly drinking herself to death. But even though we have told her so many times, I don't think she believes us. She has persistently refused treatment of any kind. Outwardly she doesn't seem to care. Inwardly she surely must hurt.

INTRODUCTION

Legal commitment was our final step after several years of faltering and stumbling. We had tried every known program developed to deal with alcoholics and their families. Many times I would rather have pushed the situation away and pretended that it didn't exist. But pretending wouldn't make the problem disappear.

Like any other disease, alcoholism can be fatal if it isn't arrested. I didn't want my mother to die; so I agreed to risk everything to stop alcoholism's deadly advance—I was even willing to take her to court.

"How did things ever get so far?" I've often agonized. "And when did my mother stop desiring to be a mother?" "How could she hurt us so much?" "And why?" "Why?" "Should I have done something differently?" "Perhaps if . . ."

Questions like these typify a family's quandary when dealing with an alcoholic. Family members often suffer more than the alcoholic initially, because while the alcoholic enjoys a private fantasy world, the family must deal with reality.

Although there is not enough evidence available to pinpoint exactly how or why a person becomes an alcoholic—not everyone who takes a drink develops a problem—the reason a person first takes a drink is an important factor in determining whether that person will become an alcoholic. Alcohol causes mood changes. It brings feelings of euphoria and causes people to feel free to say and do things they would otherwise consider inappropriate. Most people don't depend on alcohol for this feeling of freedom. But some do, and they are the ones for whom alcohol dependence could become a serious problem.

Once a person begins to reach for alcohol to capture

feelings of freedom, one or two drinks are no longer enough. It takes one more, and then another, to reach the same level of euphoria. These mood changes are actually depressing, however, not uplifting. Those who use alcohol to remove tension from difficult situations lose touch with reality and their behavior patterns become quite predictable.

They find more excuses to reach for a drink. Soon they must hide the bottles so others will not know how much they are consuming. Then they must manufacture more and more excuses for taking another drink, and then another.

If the level of alcohol consumption continues rising, physical health suffers. Food won't stay down. Vital organs begin to malfunction. Blackouts occur. Serious injury eventually results. The alcoholic either experiences a physical breakdown or injures someone else. Auto accidents caused by drunken drivers are all too common. The statistics are staggering.

Alcoholics function in a mist when drinking. Incidents happen they cannot remember. They say and do things that are strange and perverse to their personality. They injure themselves and can't remember how. And they are often locked into a denial system that will not allow them to listen to attempts to make them aware of their problem.

Physical and emotional suffering are not the only kind the alcoholic causes, however. Those who employ problem drinkers pay a high toll. Absenteeism and ineffective job performance become serious problems, and the person's inability to stay sober on the job creates potentially dangerous situations. The employer, however, cannot fire someone on suspicion alone. Evidence must be recorded, even though it may be difficult to obtain. So sometimes employers use another excuse for firing, like frequent absences, rather than reveal the actual reason.

But firing isn't always the best answer. Many employers would rather rehabilitate the person. Some have even set up rehabilitation programs at work so the alcoholic can concentrate on recovery while being assured of a job.

But alcoholism exacts its most terrible toll from the alcoholic's family. Family members make excuses for the drinking at first. They feel that if they change *their* behavior the alcoholic will stop drinking. Unbearable tension mounts as the alcoholism progresses. If a spouse drinks, the non-drinking spouse eventually will either begin drinking or leave. If children drink, they are thrown out or put away.

Research identifies several key roles played by family members dealing with alcoholism.[1] First, there is the chief enabler. This person is usually the spouse or person closest to the alcoholic. Chief enablers divide their time between covering for the alcoholic and taking the blame for the alcoholic's behavior.

Chief enablers accept responsiblity for alcoholics by seeing that they get to work on time, call in sick when they can't go in, and by making excuses for embarrassing behavior, and so on. Enablers don't realize that these actions prevent alcoholics from facing reality.

Chief enablers often take the blame for the development of the alcoholism problem, with some help from the alcoholic, of course. The alcoholic says "If only you'd be more loving" or "If only you'd spend more time with me." The enabler then excuses the drinking because the alcoholic has triggered feelings of guilt.

Enablers also offer sympathy to the alcoholic. "Your job is a rough one; you need a drink." Or "That situation sounds trying; relax and have a drink." Through these actions and excuses, chief enablers also lose touch with reality. Eventually unexpressed feelings are either suppressed, often resulting in illness, or they explode into confrontation. Anger over constant disappointments and feelings of powerlessness and inadequacy from failing to deal successfully with the alcoholic begin to mount up until enablers must make a choice. They either join in the drinking or they confront the alcoholic. Depending on how the confrontation is handled, the family either finds a solution or falls apart in divorce.

When a parent drinks, the children are usually caught in the middle. They often take on the blame without realizing the true cause of the problem. "If I become quieter or stay out of trouble (or whatever) maybe Mom won't get so upset and drink," they reason.

What kind of feelings are real to children close to alcoholics? Dr. Stephanie Brown and Claudia Black have researched this subject. Black estimates that "10 to 16 million children under 18 live in alcoholic homes."[2] Brown and Black found certain consistent feelings in the children they interviewed.

Some children feel the need to control their situations. In an effort to survive, they keep a sharp check on their feelings. Instead of bringing them to the surface, these children bury them until they feel nothing.

Many youngsters also experience guilt feelings. Children of alcoholics often believe that things might be different if they could somehow change. These children are too immature to realize this just isn't so.

Children generally fall into three or four roles in the

family other than chief enabler. One is "family hero." Family heroes, usually the oldest child, become overly responsible. Because the only trust they've learned to have is in themselves, they appear to have everything "together." They work hard, channeling their feelings into energy. They do everything humanly possible to please the alcoholic parent—but fail. They are left with hidden scars of inadequacy and low self-esteem.

The "scapegoat," another role assumed by family members of alcoholics, withdraws from the family, looking instead to peers for approval. These children often operate with a defiant, sullen attitude. They act out their deeper feelings and often withdraw from reality by becoming chemically dependent themselves. They hide the scars of fear, loneliness, and rejection.

The "lost child" in the family has also withdrawn from what's happening. But this child, by becoming super independent and aloof, retreats in a quiet way. The lost child doesn't seem to need anybody and often has a weight problem. Anger and hurt are the scars this child must try to hide.

The "mascot" develops a humorous, or clowning, attitude toward problems. Children in this category try to cheer up everyone. They attract attention by doing funny things, thereby diverting attention from the more serious problem. Mascots are often described as hyperactive. They usually receive the most attention in the family because they do the most to demand it. They carry scars of insecurity and fear.

How real are these descriptions? Surprisingly, they sound almost like the descriptions of any normal family. The most important difference, however, is the absolute silence that is practiced in families with an alcoholic member. In a normal family, one with two observant parents, children receive guidance as they encounter difficulties. The lines of communication are open. Such is not the case when an alcoholic is part of the family. There is no such thing as open communication. Also, the problems faced by families of alcoholics are almost always more traumatic and more complex than those faced by other families.

Alcoholism is a hidden disease—hidden not only by the alcoholic, but also by the family. Family members learn varying ways to cope with the situation. Denial is the most common. Silence seems to buy peace. In a deteriorating home life, such peace is very precious.

Even though family members sometimes cannot help the alcoholic, they can help themselves, because they are not alone in dealing with the problem. Statistics indicate that between nine and ten million people are alcoholics.[3] And those millions have families, friends, and employers.

Why doesn't someone stop the alcoholic before things get so bad? Often close relatives and friends do not realize that the person has lost touch with reality. And they find it easier not to talk about the drinking. Due to lack of information and education, well-meaning family members, friends, and employers often cover for alcoholics, hoping that in time they will figure things out for themselves. By doing this, however, they become the alcoholic's worst enemy. And by not acknowledging the seriousness of the situation, they become part of the problem. Families that don't realize they can play a vital role in getting the alcoholic to seek help often fail to reach out for help until it's too late.

Most of us probably know someone—a personal friend

or relative—whom we suspect has (or has had) a drinking problem. Unless we feel close to that person, however, we may never need to confront them. And even if the person we know is our spouse, parent, child, or friend, we may still choose not to confront them.

However, if we don't make an effort, the results may prove very costly, very costly indeed. We must ask ourselves if the price we pay for silence is worth it. If we decide it's not, there is something positive we can do about the problem. Help *is* available. Alcoholics *do* recover. And, more importantly to me, so do their families. By sharing my experiences, I hope to help those who are hurting in silence. "For if you continue in my work, you are truly my disciples, and you will know the truth, and the truth will set you free" (John 8:32 RSV).

1

The Alcoholic Family

We looked impishly happy in the photo. I was four and my brother was three when Mom had it taken. I'm glad I have a few joyful moments like this recorded on paper, because I haven't many in my memory. They've all been blocked out.

Erratic behavior was the first symptom we noticed in my mother. Her voice slurred on the phone, or she would laugh at inappropriate times. She stopped performing her normal activities and retreated into herself. Her walk became unsteady. Finally, we could smell the alcohol on her breath. Later we discovered her cache of bottles. We had no idea she'd been drinking so much.

I am the oldest of three children, and for as long as I can remember my mother has had a drinking problem.

As I grew older I felt more and more devastated by my circumstances. Most of all, I felt cheated.

As a little girl, I was confused and baffled by Mom's behavior. One time I would play with something and it would be OK; the next time she would react violently. But I was still too young to know that alcohol made the difference in her reactions. I soon learned to avoid confrontation by being good. I also became very sensitive to Mom's moodiness.

What is it like being the child of an alcoholic? A living nightmare. Unlike the bruises of physically abused children, the bruises of children abused psychologically and emotionally are invisible, making them almost impossible to detect and thus difficult to heal. Difficult, but not impossible.

In many ways, my family fit the pattern common to families of alcoholics. We never talked about anything that bothered us. We knew Mom had problems, but no one discussed them with us. We developed an unspoken rule that it was best to ignore Mom's behavior, as though we wouldn't have to deal with it if we didn't talk about it.

In other ways, my family did not fit the pattern. My mother did not physically abuse us. Considering her condition many times, she might unknowingly have done so. She even tried to keep a semblance of normal life, at least in the beginning.

By the time I was ten, I treated my mother as a sick person. I explained to my friends that she had a serious illness and that was why they couldn't come to my house to play. I didn't dare let them see her in her condition. I made excuses for her inability to attend school functions or programs or other parent activities by pleading her "illness." I covered for her.

My mother embarrassed me. She didn't bother to take care of herself and would appear at a function with hair uncombed, clothes a disaster, and without makeup. Weaving to a chair, she might find it or she might fall. The humiliation of these experiences felt worse than the hurt when she didn't show up at all.

I became very skilled at hiding my feelings. After a while, things didn't hurt so much. I even began to believe the excuses I'd made up for Mom. I never actually saw her drinking from a bottle, so I couldn't be sure that's what her problem was.

My father, frustrated after ten years of trying every potential solution, finally left. And by leaving Mom, he left my brothers and me to face a different set of problems and a new range of emotions, which I continued to handle the way I'd learned would be safest—by retreating into silence.

During the divorce and after, my father tried to gain custody of my brothers and me, but proving my mother unfit was very difficult to do. Like many alcoholics, she had become very clever at hiding evidence. The judge left the choice to the children.

I faced a heart-rending decision. Could we continue living with Mom under these difficult conditions? Could we live with the consequences of leaving? If my brothers and I left Mom, I truly believed she would die. I simply could not live with that on my conscience.

So, as the oldest child, I insisted, not once or twice, but on several occasions, that we preferred living with our mother. I never told anyone how I really felt. And, after years of practice, I was very good at hiding my feelings, even from myself. Since no one knew my fears and thoughts, no one could reassure me or correct my faulty thinking. I thought I was doing my mother a favor, but I was wrong.

After Dad left, Mom's condition worsened until she couldn't even get out of bed. She consumed only alcohol, so she became physically sick. I assumed the role of family hero for good. At age ten I cooked, cleaned, washed, and cared for my two brothers, Mom, and myself. No one knew the extent to which I covered for my mother. I sacrificed my social life to keep my family together.

Visits with Dad and other family members were the highlight of our life. We spent several weeks in the summer with my father and his new wife, during which time we had a taste of real family life. And my mother's mother and aunt, Maybelle, who lived together near us, provided the only consistent, loving atmosphere we knew. My grandmother would sometimes take us to Mom's sister's home for a week or two. These were delightfully happy experiences, but it was very difficult to go back home again. We realized what we were missing. But without such havens of care, our plight would have been even more desperate.

During this time, perhaps because no one realized, or wanted to realize, how serious Mom's problem was, no one from her family tried to force her to seek help. I never discussed the problem with anyone because my mother became very ugly whenever anyone suggested things weren't OK. As she got worse, she became abusive if she thought we had talked to anyone about her. So we avoided confrontation by simply shutting up.

Even Aunt Maybelle, who herself had been an alcoholic and was very close to Mom, refused to accept the facts. Perhaps she found it too painful to admit that more than one person in the family could have this devastating problem. To help my mother, the family may have had to deal with their own past relationships, which they apparently were not prepared to do.

I was locked in a constant battle. Part of me wanted to deal with the problem, and part of me wanted to pretend it wasn't there. The silent part won. I developed a wall of protection from the hurt. I shut myself off from any feelings at all. I didn't have any close friends, and I carried a chip on my shoulder that seemed more like a log.

I was growing up to be a bitter, frustrated, angry, hurt young woman—until I met someone who changed me and drastically changed my circumstances.

2

God Reaches Down

Our standard of living was at rock bottom. Much of the money my father sent supported my mother's drinking habit. I was frustrated trying to make ends meet. Sometimes I was even forced to steal or beg food to feed the family. I couldn't afford popular style clothes or make-up, and I had no one to teach me proper grooming. I stood out like a sore thumb in school. But I pretended I didn't care when my classmates teased me. I had no social life. The few invitations that anyone issued, I had to refuse. I didn't dare leave my mother alone. Life had become intolerable. And I was only fifteen.

On my way to school one morning, I was hit by a car. Terrified that someone would find out about my home life, I refused to tell anyone. But the next day one teacher noticed me wincing and had the school nurse take me to the emergency room. X-rays revealed a badly bruised and swollen wrist, which took six weeks to heal. Having my arm treated was a welcome relief, but greater relief came when I learned that my mother had not been drunk when school authorities called to tell her what happened.

Since we could not afford a doctor, my frequent sore throats went unattended. And if anyone else in the family was sick, I had to stay home and nurse them. In spite of excessive absences from school, however, I was able to maintain a high grade point average.

But I was becoming more and more silent and introspective. I resented the life that had been imposed on me. I hated all the extra work. I was lonely. No one understood my problems. Most of my classmates led normal lives in two-parent homes. They didn't have to cope with circumstances far beyond their ability to handle.

The months and years took their toll. I decided I had nothing to look forward to. No one cared whether I lived or died. I could envision no future. Somewhat melodramatically, I decided to punish my parents for the terrible hurts they'd inflicted on me. I would commit suicide.

My mother consumed more alcohol than she did food, so she suffered from a host of illnesses and kept several medications handy for treating her many physical problems. I knew that if I took enough of her pills I would die. I could count on Mom being too drunk to do anything. And my brothers were too young to figure out what was happening until it was too late. I'd show them all!

I waited until everyone had gone to bed before taking Mom's pills to my room to solve my problems once and for all. I stood in front of the mirror, glancing from the bottle of pills in my hand to my reflection in the mirror, debating. As I struggled within myself, the words a friend had spoken weeks earlier drifted back.

Only one classmate had shown an interest in me. He tried breaking through my barriers by inviting me to several Youth for Christ rallies. I finally went. Driving back, he asked me, "What would happen if you died tonight? Would you go to heaven or fall into eternal nothingness?"

"I don't know," I replied. Nor did I care. I'd never been to church before. I felt God would want to take care of me because of the good things I had done. I had no assurances of my beliefs, however.

My friend admonished me to think about it. I promised I would—someday.

As I gazed back into the mirror, his question raced through my mind. What *would* happen if I died tonight? Would anyone care? Looking closely in the mirror, I saw the harsh lines, the sullen mouth, the bitterness. I felt despondent. In spite of all the sacrifices I'd made, no one really cared about me. And I'd been so wrapped up in my own problems that I had failed to think of anyone else.

Then other words I'd heard came back to me. "Somebody cares. God cares. His Son died for one such as you."

"So what?" I shouted back at the face in the mirror. "Who asked Him to? Why should He care?"

"Because God loves all His creation," I remembered hearing someone say. "He made you, and He loves you. Why not give God a chance to show you His love?"

"How, God?" I cried out. "What can you do? You can't change my mother or my circumstances, can you?"

"No," I heard, "but God can change you and your attitudes if you'll give Him a chance."

I realized that night how miserable I was. Deep in my heart, though, I knew I did not want to die. What I wanted was a new life. I had heard that the power of Christ could make me a new creation. Maybe it was worth a try. Certainly things could not get much worse.

That very night, with stumbling words, I agreed to give God's way a chance. Through the ministering of God's Holy Spirit, I asked Jesus to forgive my sins and invited Him to take charge of my life. For the first time in years I slept peacefully.

With God's help, I determined a new course of action. Instead of waiting for people to come to me, I would reach out to them. I knew that approach would work. I had reached out to God, and He had answered me. I tried smiling and greeting everyone I met. I opened the conversation first. Instead of concentrating on myself, I became interested in others.

I began to read the Bible. I took the words of Matthew 19:19 to heart: "You shall love your neighbor as yourself." As God taught me to love myself, He showed me how to love others.

The results astounded me. People responded to my smiles. At the end of the school year I received the school's hospitality award. The most unpopular girl had become the friendliest, thanks to God.

Entrusting my life to Christ meant I could turn my problems over to Him. He cared about me, so He cared about my troubles as well. My life needed a miracle, so I prayed for one.

My miracle came several months later when my aunt finally accepted the reality of Mom's condition and forced her to sign herself in for alcoholic rehabilitation. I never knew exactly what happened, since no one talked about where Mom went when she was hospitalized. One day I came home, and she was gone; a few weeks later she returned, and she had stopped drinking.

We never talked about where she had been or what had happened. Her drinking was no longer an issue. And I feared that talking about it would make her feel guilty and perhaps send her back to the bottle. She had quit, and that was good enough for me.

Life became more normal. Mom resumed most of her responsibilities, including her role as family authority. I resented this at first. After all, I'd been on my own for years. But I was so glad to be free from my many responsibilities that my resentment didn't last long.

I matured as a Christian believer and trusted God's guidance. After graduating from high school, I left home to attend a Christian college. While pursuing my teaching degree, I met a fine Christian man. A year later we married and settled in Florida. Living 1500 miles from home, I began a new life with my own family. I felt like Cinderella. I was going to live happily ever after.

God continued to work on healing my memories. One at a time, Jesus walked with me back through the scenes of my childhood and stood with me there. He radiated light into the darkest corners of each one and released my fears and angry feelings.

But eventually God asked me to forgive my mother for those painful scenes. "Honor thy father and mother," I read while studying the Ten Commandments. Not mine, I thought. Surely God did not expect me to honor *my* parents!

In a state of righteous indignation, I was certain God must make exceptions. But the fourth commandment didn't mention any. God said honor them. He didn't add,

"If they treat you well," or "If they're wonderful." He just said do it.

I later came across Martin Luther's explanation of the fourth commandment:

> We should fear and love God, that we may not despise them (our parents) to anger, but give them honor, serve and obey them, and hold them in love and esteem.[1]

I had learned to take God's commandments seriously. If He said I must do this, then I must find out how. How could I love and esteem my mother after what she had done?

Wrestling within, I spent a long time in prayer. Finally I agreed to try—just try—to do what God asked. I pleaded with Him to show me one lovable thing about my mother.

He did. "Here, take my glasses for a while," He said. "Look and see what I see." Instead of all the bad things I had always seen in my mother, I began to see the good in her. I realized how much I appreciated her ability to listen to me. I could talk for hours, and she always sat down and listened. Then I saw her beautiful smile. Mom has a great sense of humor. And above all, she beat her alcoholism, which took courage. The more I looked, the more I found. I would never see her in the same way again.

My past became a blank. Forgiving and learning to love my mother allowed me to experience what 2 Corinthians 5:17 promises: "Therefore, if any one is in Christ, he is a new creation; the old has passed away, behold, the new has come" (RSV). The past disappeared and would never haunt me again. I was free. What a glorious feeling!

During the next ten years, as I concentrated on my

mother's genuine beauty, I succeeded in establishing a new, rich foundation for a sharing relationship with her.

My own family increased as my husband and I had three children. We visited Mom almost every summer. She took a nursing job and became involved in a new career for herself. The world beamed bright and beautiful. The foundation of our relationship finally seemed secure. Little did I know that it was built on sand.

3

Plunging Backward

I still remember clearly everything that happened the day my brother Bruce called. He and his family lived near my mother, 1500 miles from us. We visited in the summer, wrote frequently, but seldom called each other. I knew what he had to say must be important or he would have written or called in the evening, not at lunchtime.

I felt the dread creeping through my body when he said, "You're never going to believe this . . . " I was afraid to hear what he was about to say.

"You were right," he continued. "Mother is drinking again. And she's taken a serious fall and broken her arm."

I cringed. I'd been concerned about Mom for several months, ever since Aunt Maybelle, to whom Mom had been very close, died after a long bout with cancer. Mom had been her constant companion during her illness. Although Mom seemed composed throughout the funeral, I wasn't convinced. I feared that she might break down when there was no one around to help her.

Shortly after the funeral, Mom's letters stopped coming. She never wrote long letters, but I looked forward to hearing the family news every other week. Her silence bothered me.

A month or so later I convinced Mom to come down for a visit. She looked thinner and tired, and she wouldn't say much when I pressed her about how she was doing. She explained that her job had demanded many hours during the recent holidays. I was satisfied with her answer.

But then, when we were out for dinner one evening, Mom ordered a glass of wine. I hadn't seen her drink in twelve years. Fear settled in the pit of my stomach. I soon rationalized, however, that she was entitled to enjoy herself. An occasional drink didn't give me the right to assume she had a problem.

Silence once again became the predominant factor in our lives. I was afraid to talk to my mother about that one drink, so I let the incident pass without comment. But something inside nagged me. I couldn't get rid of the feeling that something was wrong.

At home that summer, I was surprised to see Mom having a beer at a family outing. And on another day she ordered a glass of wine while dining out. Watching her become giddy, I realized things had changed. When I casually mentioned I was surprised to see her take a drink, she pointed out that the rest of us all enjoyed a social drink occasionally. Why shouldn't she?

Instead of pressing the issue, I asked my brothers to keep an eye on her. Richard lived in town and saw her weekly; Bruce saw her about once a month. I explained that I thought Mom was lonely and maybe it would be good if they could check in a little more often. Even in talking to my brothers, I couldn't voice my suspicions. I was too afraid they were true.

Although I had suspected, I was not prepared for what Bruce told me when he called four months later. I had no idea the problem could become so serious so quickly. As he described their observations over the past four months and their discovery of bottles in Mom's apartment, I cried. Emotionally I was plunged back fifteen years.

I didn't know how to answer my brother's questions. All I could say was, "I'll call back later." I hung up the phone and called out to God. Through my tears I cried, "Help me, Lord. Give me some words of encouragement before I fall apart."

Verses I had recently studied immediately came to my mind. "We know that in everything God works for good with those who love Him . . ." (Rom. 8:28 RSV). Then I thought of 1 Peter 1:6–7. "In this you rejoice, though now for a little while you may have to suffer various trials, so that the genuineness of your faith, more precious than gold which though perishable is tested by fire, may redound to praise and glory and honor at the revelation of Jesus Christ" (RSV).

God sent me a message. He was telling me to keep my eyes on Him as things began to happen. He reassured me that this testing would make me like refined gold. I couldn't predict what would happen or envision where this experience would lead. I could only count on God's promise to be with me, to lead and guide me, and to increase my faith if I would trust Him. Those thoughts later sustained me through some of the darkest hours I'd ever faced.

I began to pray, asking God for wisdom and direction. I knew I needed more information before taking action, so I contacted the local chapter of the National Council on Alcoholism. I received a wealth of pamphlets from them, but since programs vary from state to state, I found out very little about what might be available to help my mother.

To avoid the frustrations of working from such a long distance away, I decided to fly home and get first-hand information. My brothers worked, so they didn't have the time or opportunity to investigate the possibilities. And, as big sister, it was natural for me to take charge. I didn't realize I was slipping back into my role as family hero.

I talked to Mom's employer as soon as I arrived back in town. Admitting to a stranger that my mother had a drinking problem was humiliating and painful, and I hoped that Mom wouldn't lose her job because of my actions. I also hoped that her employer, as a result of my honesty with him, would pressure Mom into seeking help. In talking with people at the National Council on Alcoholism, I had learned that many employers subscribe to alcoholism rehabilitation programs for employees with drinking problems. Employees can continue working while attending out-patient programs. If hospitalization is required, their job is kept open. The key to commitment, however, lies in the employer's hands.

Unfortunately, my quest was unsuccessful. Those in the medical profession often hesitate to admit that they or their colleagues have problems with alcohol. They are supposed to heal, not suffer from problems themselves.

Mom's boss said he would talk to her and suggest she seek help. He admitted, however, that the lack of evidence made him powerless to force her. They had suspected Mom had problems, but they were unable to prove anything.

I felt like pushing for something more, but once again silence won. Suppose my honesty cost Mom her job? How would she support herself? More importantly, would my actions push her beyond the limits of reality? Perhaps it would be best, I reasoned, to abandon this avenue of approach.

I needed some professional advice, so I called the Alcoholism Council in my home town to obtain the number of Alcoholics Anonymous. I asked if they had someone who could help us confront Mom about her drinking. Their answer left me feeling helpless. They would come only if Mom called them herself. I was angry. Why would Mom call when she wouldn't even admit she had a problem?

After two strikeouts, I desperately needed spiritual counseling. I had recently heard the pastor of a nearby church speak at a convention, so I called him to inquire about a Christian counselor. I knew I would feel more comfortable talking with someone who understood my point of view.

With the names and phone numbers of four counselors in my hand, I began dialing. After several calls, though, I still hadn't located one who was available on Saturday. I had to fly back on Monday. I wanted to accomplish something before I left. My frustration mounted. I pleaded with God in the phone booth. "What now? How will I handle this?"

Professionals can be a great help, but God reminded

me I didn't need anyone but Him. Ultimately God, not a counselor, would make the difference. All believers have access to the power of the living God. My job was to arm myself for battle. When I was ready, God would fight alongside me.

My brothers and I met that evening to plan our strategy. We would confront Mom, armed with the limited information we had about her behavior, and try to convince her that she needed treatment.

Arriving unexpectedly the next afternoon, we caught Mom off-guard. She tried locking herself in her room, but we stood firmly in the doorway. We finally convinced her to come downstairs and simply listen to us.

For three hours we moved through a maze of emotions. We accused her; she protested; we responded angrily; she became belligerent. At one point I became so frustrated that I cried. The experience was exhausting, but for the first time in our lives we talked to each other about the problem. Mom finally agreed she had a problem. She also admitted we needed help just to talk about it. But where could we go for that help? She would see a counselor, but she absolutely refused to be admitted to a hospital. Because it was Saturday, none of the counselors I called were available. In desperation I dialed the number of a crisis hotline and explained our problem. They arranged a meeting with a counselor for the next day.

My brothers and I left Mom's house feeling somewhat successful. We hoped she wouldn't get drunk that night. Just in case she needed sobering up the next morning, I planned to arrive early to pick her up.

When I arrived I was surprised to find Mom dressed and ready to go. But I was more surprised by what happened later. The counselor we met with was very capable, and she was able to convince Mom to express her personal feelings. I realized I had no idea how Mom had felt all these years. Some of the things she brought up astounded me. She told me, for example, that she did not enjoy it when my family visited her. I'd been inconsiderate, she said, for thinking she liked to have us around. Her apartment was too small for all of us, and our visits exhausted her.

In turn, my brothers and I expressed our feelings about her drinking, and she too was surprised at our reaction. In this atmosphere of non-confrontation, Mom agreed to try an out-patient program at a local hospital. I was disappointed that the crisis counselor wasn't equipped to deal with long-term solutions and served only as a temporary aid, because Mom related to her very well. But my feeling that we had finally accomplished something positive outweighed my slight disappointment.

I flew home with high hopes for success. My brother had agreed to drive Mom to the sessions; Mom had agreed to attend them. What could go wrong?

4

Moving Out in Faith

I soon realized we had been duped. Mom went to the rehabilitation program twice, then decided she didn't like the counselor nor the treatment. She refused to continue. By agreeing to try rehabilitation, she had placated us. She had succeeded in getting us off her back for a while.

I wondered what would have happened if we had been more forceful that Saturday morning at Mom's house. If we had pressured her, would she have agreed to check herself into a hospital? I berated myself for my foolishness. We should never have given her the time to think (and drink) and reconsider.

But the past was just that, and the future was what I needed to concern myself with. During the next several months Mom's condition worsened. She fell again, badly injuring her knee. I would try calling her for several days and not receive an answer. Living so far away I felt helpless.

Once again I began to assume an obligation for my mother. I believed Mom would let me help her if only I could be there. My husband and I began praying and discussing our options. Finally, convinced it was the only way I would experience peace again, we decided to try and move back home.

The next six months were filled with indecision. We closed up our house in Miami, as we did each summer, and I packed what I thought the children might need for school that fall. I believed my husband would find a job up north, and I wanted to be prepared.

I refused to worry about details like selling the house and saying good-bye to friends. I believed God would take care of everything when the proper time came. Our first task was for one of us to find a job.

My husband, a guidance counselor, got some good leads on several job openings, which are not very plentiful in that profession, and made application. After several appointments and interviews, a couple of the opportunities looked very promising. We just had to wait. The suspense was almost unbearable.

In the meantime I applied for teaching positions in nearby areas. Principals were reluctant to hire me, however, as my husband was not yet employed.

We were both so busy job hunting that summer that I hardly saw Mom. I didn't need many excuses to avoid her. She was no longer trying to hide her condition.

"Grandma acted awful funny," my daughter observed after one visit. We could hear Mom giggling inside the house, but she refused to unlock the door and let us in. I

MOVING OUT IN FAITH 35

suddenly realized that my mother's behavior affected not only me but my children as well.

Mom's behavior at restaurants was embarrassing, and her weaving and giddiness at home elicited more comments and questions from my children. I could not bring myself to tell them the truth about their grandmother, however. The patterns of the past began to emerge as I made up excuses for Mom. Several times I cut our visits short to avoid further unpleasantness.

In spite of my embarrassment and anger, however, I wanted to prove to my mother that we loved and cared for her. I continued visiting but, as in the past, avoided the subject of her drinking. However, it still stood between us, and we both knew it.

As summer faded, so did my hopes of moving north. None of our job opportunities worked out, so we were forced to return to Miami before school started. My spirits drooped. I had been so certain God wanted us to move. How could I help Mom from 1500 miles away? What was God doing to me?

I had wanted desperately to move, not only for Mom but for myself. Ever since moving to Miami, I had suffered terribly from allergies. My allergist agreed that a cooler climate might make me feel better.

Also, the neighborhood we lived in had gradually changed. We watched the population change from eighty percent white to eighty percent black. I was unconcerned at first. Our new neighbors were not much different from our old ones. But when our children started school, they experienced problems. Being a minority took its toll. Our oldest daughter came home crying every day because she couldn't take the teasing and cruel comments from the other children. I had little hope that the situation would ever improve.

In addition, I was concerned about prolonged separation from my family. Although Roger's parents lived nearby, my own parents hardly knew their grandchildren. My brothers knew my children only casually; we barely knew theirs. I knew the gap would get larger in the future as our children developed more interests. Soon they would be unwilling to spend every summer away from their Miami friends. I would then be unable to visit home, and my family would drift further and further apart.

While living in Florida, many of our Christian friends had replaced absent family members. We had developed many beautiful relationships. But having learned how to enjoy such close relationships, I wanted to go home and rebuild my own family. God taught me so much, and I was eager to share it with them.

Behind all my concerns for health and family relationships, however, ran one constant thread of thought: Perhaps my family could become instrumental in Mom's recovery if only we lived closer. If she was presented with the living example of Christ, I believed she could find her way back. It was a risk I was willing to take.

Roger and I started praying again. Nothing had yet happened to change my mind about moving. Even though things hadn't worked out the first time, I wasn't ready to give up. I had to be certain about God's answer, and I knew there were ways to find out for sure.

In February we decided to test the Lord by reversing the process we had tried the previous year. We put our house up for sale. If it sold, we reasoned, we would know God wanted us to leave. If it didn't, we'd stay. To prove to ourselves that we were seeking God's will and not our own selfish desires, we decided to make selling the house as difficult as possible. We priced it very high. Interest rates were beginning to escalate, and many houses in our area were for sale. Someone would have to want our house very much to be willing to pay the price we were asking.

To make it even more difficult, we insisted that no "for sale" sign be posted in our yard. We also indicated that we wanted no advertising other than the multiple listing of realtors. Our realtor was quite perturbed by our demands and warned us that we were making things very difficult.

Most other homes in our area were taking one to two years to sell, so we knew God would have to intervene if ours was to sell sooner. We were expecting a miracle; our realtor was not. So he was the most surprised when, just three weeks later, we received an excellent offer—in cash, no less. We didn't have to wait for an approval from the mortgage company to close the deal. I felt as though God was trying to get our attention by doing something unbelievable. It worked!

Three months later we put our belongings into storage and headed north. We had taken the first big step of faith by selling our house, but we still faced the seemingly impossible task of finding a job.

I suppose I shouldn't have been surprised when, three weeks later, my husband signed a contract. He stumbled on a guidance job that had been open since the previous May. Because it involved servicing five rural communities, others hadn't considered it.

After Roger got the job, God continued to remove obstacles. His certification in Florida was in secondary counseling, so it looked as though he could only be granted a temporary license for the elementary schools he would service. In checking his records, however, school authorities discovered that he had earned the credentials for elementary counseling as well.

In addition, his school in Miami granted him a leave of absence, so we didn't have to burn all our bridges behind us. I could find out if my health would improve in a colder climate and do what I could to help my mother, but if things didn't work out we could return to the security of Miami.

Our excitement mounted as we watched all the puzzle pieces being fit into place. We truly believed God held us in the palm of His hand.

Housing was our final obstacle. Finding a place to rent big enough for five people in a rural community would not be easy. Would God provide once more, or would the entire project fail because we could not find a suitable place to live?

The first day we looked we met a realtor who had an old home he was thinking of renting. It belonged to his elderly aunt, who had fallen in the winter and been confined to a nursing home. We looked at it the same afternoon. It had plenty of space for a growing family, but it was quite different from our Florida home, which was much newer. And we were concerned about how warm it would be in the winter. The realtor gave us a week to think things over.

As we checked further we found that God had again provided beautifully for us. The elementary school our children would attend was just across the street. And though the community was small compared to Miami, it had all we needed. Everything was within walking distance, so buying a second car would be unnecessary. The only major drawback was that my mother lived thirty miles away. But thirty was certainly better than 1500.

Within six months, with God's help, we had accomplished the impossible. Everything had gone so smoothly we hadn't even had many moments of worry. God had planned everything to the smallest detail. The experience taught us some tremendous lessons in trust, but I still had no idea how valuable those lessons would become.

I was excited as I anticipated what God had in store for us next, and I was anxious to begin working with Mom.

5

Programs Designed to Help

Mom suffered another serious fall while we were moving. She broke several bones in her back and could hardly move. A neighbor, who became suspicious because the lights in Mom's house hadn't been turned on for a few days, finally found Mom three days after her accident.

My brothers took her to the hospital and advised the doctors of her alcoholism. They ordered further tests, which revealed signs of cirrhosis of the liver. We needed to get her into treatment—soon!

Once again I called the local chapter of the National Council on Alcoholism to find out about available programs. We had already tried crisis counseling and conventional programs, without success. We needed a way to convince Mom that she needed help.

I drove out to a private agency that had a program designed to work with alcoholics and their families and spent several hours with one of their counselors. He helped me understand how a person becomes chemically dependent and explained about roles family members play. He asked me if I recognized myself in any of the roles, and I explained to him where I used to fit.

"But my faith has taught me how to forgive my mother and forget the past," I added. "I no longer recall, nor care to remember it. Now my concern centers on Mom's present drinking problem."

"But you need help as much as your mother does," he insisted. "After all, your mother's drinking isn't your problem. You need help in learning how to deal with her, but you're not responsible for curing her. You should be more concerned about yourself than about her."

As a Christian, I couldn't accept his theory. Because I loved Mom, I believed it was my business to help her in any way I could. I was no longer fulfilling the role of my childhood. I had broken my walls of silence by talking to Mom and others about her drinking. I rejected the idea that I should give up trying to help her.

I explained to him why I was so certain I could help Mom if only I could convince her she needed it. "While we were living in Miami," I told him, "God brought several people into my life who, like Mom, had negative self-images. They needed practical help as well as prayer. As they received both, I watched them flower under His loving care. One brought her son through a drug crisis. One lost a job and found an exciting new career. Another failed in school, changed careers, then became successful. Another family was reunited. Roger and I could have ignored their needs, but we believe 'love your neighbor as yourself' applies to us. And we also believe that what worked for those people can work for Mom—if we can just get through to her."

The counselor congratulated me on my overcoming faith. He seemed amazed that I didn't fit the pattern of most family heroes. I hadn't married an alcoholic or become one myself, and I enjoyed a healthy relationship with my husband and children.

"Give me a call if you convince your mother to get treatment," he said as I was leaving, "or if you decide you need help for yourself."

With a smaller checkbook balance and more frustration than ever, I walked slowly to my car. He hadn't offered me one single suggestion as to how to convince Mom she needed treatment.

On my way home I remembered reading *Pathfinders* by Gail Sheehy and what she said about people like me who have successfully overcome obstacles. According to Sheehy, one of the major components in the success of these pathfinders is faith.[1] I was not surprised, of course, but knowing that research backs up my experiences was somehow reassuring, especially after my dismal encounter with an "expert."

A few weeks later I heard about a Christian counseling service at a nearby church and called to investigate. At least we would speak the same language, I told myself. Perhaps they could put me on the right track.

The counselor I met with gave me the encouragement I needed. He assured me that the healing and forgiveness I had experienced were indeed very real. He understood the power of Christ's forgiving love and, unlike the previous counselor, knew that the past could be put aside forever. He agreed that the problem was my mother's, not mine, and helped me put everything into perspective. "Prioritize your difficulties and plan a course of action," he advised. His answer was simple, yet I felt as though I'd received a breath of fresh air.

Although he wasn't trained to counsel alcoholics specifically, he offered to meet with Mom and me to help convince her to seek help. He recommended another program for her actual treatment.

In my excitement, I drove directly to Mom's house. I wanted to get everything off my chest while I still had some courage. We talked casually at first. Then I noticed something peculiar. Tucked under the edge of the pillow Mom sat on, just barely visible, was a bottle. Suddenly I wanted to laugh. What a ludicrous situation. Here we were, chatting normally, while my mother sat on her bottle. Did she think she could fool me?

Something inside me suddenly snapped. Did I have a right to disturb Mom's fantasy world? After all, it was her life, and she chose to drink. If she was happy, wouldn't it be simpler to let her alone?

I began to doubt. Maybe I really was the one who had the problem. Instead of approaching Mom about seeing a counselor with me, I kept on chattering. Awhile later I left, never having mustered up the courage to break Mom's happy mood.

Several days later I wrote Mom a note telling her I had a problem and wished we could go together to see a counselor about it. I promised not to hound her about going, one yes or no would do. She never gave me an answer, so we continued to play the charade.

I settled back and let things rest awhile, waiting for God to act again. I wasn't idle, however. I continued to accumulate information about local programs and talked again with the people at Alcoholics Anonymous. Since Mom wouldn't go with me to talk with them, I thought perhaps one of them would go with me to talk to her. Yes, they assured me, someone could go, but Mom had to call them herself.

Earlier I was angry about such an answer, but now I understood the reason behind it. Unless the person recognized the need for help, talking would be a waste of time. I had proven that myself. But how long would I have to wait for Mom to reach out? Couldn't I do something to keep her from killing herself?

To answer my questions, the A.A. counselor put me in touch with an Al-Anon group, a non-denominational organization formed specifically for families of alcoholics. Most well-populated areas have one.

Unfortunately, there was no such group in our small community, and the nearest city was too far away for me to travel for weekly meetings. My brother, however, joined an Al-Anon group and found it very helpful. It provided him an opportunity to express the frustrations and difficulties family members face. Following guidelines similar to those developed by Alcoholics Anonymous, the organization stresses Christian principles. Family members are urged to concentrate on their own behavior, not on the alcoholic's. And group support encourages members to try different ways to minimize the influence the alcoholic has on the family.

> The Al-Anon Family Groups are a fellowship of relatives and friends of alcoholics who share their experience, strength and hope in order to solve their common problems. We believe alcoholism is a family illness and that changed attitudes can aid recovery.

Al-Anon is not allied with any sect, denomination, political entity, organization or institution; does not engage in any controversy, neither endorses nor opposes any cause. There are no dues for membership. Al-Anon is self-supporting through its own voluntary contributions.

Al-Anon has but one purpose: to help families of alcoholics. We do this by practicing the Twelve Steps, by welcoming and giving comfort to families of alcoholics and by giving understanding and encouragement to the alcoholic.[2]

Even though such a group was not available in my area, I knew the importance of sharing with a support group. For years I was part of a prayer group in Miami. It had been easy for me to share my deepest feelings with fellow Christians who supported me with love and prayer. Working through rough times was much easier in the presence of caring people. The importance of loving support in a crisis cannot be overemphasized.

During my search I also became aware of a new support group called Alcoholics Victorious.[3] Their creed is based on 2 Corinthians 5:17. As their name implies, they believe alcoholics, with the power of Christ, can be victorious in overcoming alcohol. Speakers address the groups weekly. Even though the programs are directed to the alcoholic personally, I was encouraged to know that such groups exist.

In continuing my search, I learned how a person is committed to the local state hospital for alcoholics, what it costs, and how the program operates. But again, unless Mom would sign herself in the program would be ineffective. My problem still was how to get her there. When I asked how, I got answers from "I don't know" to "Drag her there."

My confusion was unbearable. In desperation I called another branch of the National Council on Alcoholism, one closer to my home. For nearly an hour I spilled out my frustration to the woman on the other end of the line.

"Why don't you read *I'll Quit Tomorrow*[4] by Dr. Vernon Johnson?" she finally suggested. "He talks about ways the family can get the alcoholic to treatment. It might be the answer. I'd be happy to order it for you."

When the book arrived I couldn't put it down. At last I'd found someone who understood. Dr. Johnson had some of the answers I'd been searching for. Families don't have to wait until the situation is impossible before taking action, he said. His words were just the balm I needed.

He outlined a procedure called "family intervention," which he uses at his hospital in Minneapolis, Minnesota. Using this technique, the commitment rate is seventy-five percent. As I read further, I remembered hearing that Betty Ford's family had successfully tried a similar process. I was excited. Here was something successful that was exactly what I had been seeking.

I began to inquire about the availability of such a program in our area. Now that I knew what to ask for, getting an answer was much simpler. Although the treatment was fairly new, one hospital in the area practiced the intervention technique. I called and got the basic information.

The best time to try intervention, Dr. Johnson recommended, is during a crisis. The alcoholic, already under outside pressure, responds better. It's easier to cut through his or her defenses in such a time of stress. When my mother had a crisis, and she would, we ought to be prepared to reach her.

I sifted through the information for a few days and talked things over with my brothers. They would both play an important role in this procedure. Armed with our new information and encouraged by a new strategy, we sat back to await Mom's inevitable crisis. A month later our opportunity came.

6

Intervention

On New Year's Day Mom's employer phoned me. Mom had arrived at work smashed the previous night, and her boss had fired her on the spot. We had our crisis. Without a job, Mom could drink all day. But what would she do when her money ran out? The timing gave us a perfect opportunity. It was now or, perhaps, never.

I called the hospital and explained the new developments. I knew we needed professional help if we were going to capitalize on Mom's crisis. Because alcoholics often become defensive, those dealing with them must be prepared to dig in. To overcome the alcoholic's defenses requires a soldier's training. I knew I had to prepare as carefully as for a battle. If I was caught with my own defenses down I could lose the battle, and perhaps even the war.

I found out the time and place of the first meeting and decided to drive up for it. My training program started with a six-night orientation called "Family Education Series." At first I rebelled at the rigorous schedule because I felt I already knew quite a bit about alcoholism. However, when I arrived and found the room packed, I realized why it was necessary. I had taken two years to gather my information. These people would get it all in six weeks.

During the first two sessions medical professionals explained the disease and the forms it takes. The next two sessions focused on the roles of family members in the progress of the disease, and the last two sessions were devoted to the discussion of intervention techniques. Each session lasted about two hours—a one-hour lecture followed by at least an hour of discussion.

After attending the education series, those who were interested in trying intervention could make an appointment to meet with a counselor for four additional sessions. A rehearsal meeting was scheduled next, and then finally, after twelve weeks of being intensely involved in bringing the alcoholic to reality, came the actual day of intervention.

My brothers had agreed to join me in this effort, so they also needed the training. Since Bruce lived 90 miles away, we arranged a similar training program with a private counselor in his area. Richard met me at the local hospital on the first night of the series. Together, fearfully, we walked in.

Any time one sets out into unfamiliar territory there is an element of fear. We had no way of knowing what to expect. I believed God had brought us to this time and place and that He would see us through safely, but I did not know how strongly I would begin to question this belief.

As the lecturer covered the roles of family members, Richard and I easily identified the parts we played as children. Though not as strongly, we still played them as adults. Then the instructor showed us a film entitled "If You Loved Me." Right there in front of us we watched scenes from our own childhood reenacted. Although my childhood memories were dimmer since the Lord had released me from their burden, many of the feelings were still with me. And for my brother, the pain was fresh. He had been too young to remember much. But as I watched him respond to the film, I knew he had begun to remember. For both of us the emotional pain was almost unbearable. We squeezed one another's hand and cried together. I knew the healing process had begun for him.

Our first training session was also our last. Mom hit her crisis. We had to accelerate our actions to capitalize on the timing. We couldn't wait eleven or more weeks to get ready. We had four at the most.

I made our first appointment with our counselors, a man and a woman who specialized in intervention. Their positive attitude and encouragement helped keep us from being overwhelmed by all that was happening. They took down all the pertinent information about Mom's problem and explained in detail about the intervention process. They answered all our questions, including one that was foremost on our minds—cost. Although we would have found the money if we'd had to, none of us had much ready cash. We were relieved to learn that most of the charges would be covered by my brother's insurance.

The counselors closed the session by asking us to list all the specific incidents we could remember that involved Mom's drinking and to bring the list with us the following week. They also encouraged us to find more people to include in the process, because our chances of getting through to Mom increased with the number of people involved. We would be following the guidelines listed in *I'll Quit Tomorrow* by Vernon Johnson.[1]

1. Meaningful persons must present facts.
2. Use specific events or conditions.
3. Non-judgmental tone prevails in the sessions.
4. Offer the person the opportunity to be part of the decision. Give them options.

Since our success would depend on how closely we followed these guidelines, we began looking for other "meaningful persons" in Mom's life who would help us present facts.

First we tried Mom's sister. She refused. Like us, she had tried talking with Mom without success, and she doubted this new process would work any better. I understood how she felt.

Next we talked to Mom's neighborhood friend. Unfortunately, she didn't drive and couldn't get to the hospital for the training sessions. Even if someone could have provided transportation, she couldn't take time off from her job. She also seemed a little afraid of getting involved. Again, I understood.

The counselors had told us that employers are the most effective in interventions. But Mom's employer had recently fired her, so I doubted that he would cooperate.

There was no one else to try. We discussed bringing in our children, but decided against it. The oldest was eleven, and we felt they were all too young to understand. That left my two brothers, myself, and my husband. We hoped the four of us could succeed.

My husband, Roger, couldn't attend the sessions with us because he couldn't take that much time off from work. But his emotional support was invaluable. I would never have gotten involved in the intervention program if he hadn't agreed one hundred percent. It was important to our marriage and our future family life to get this situation settled.

In the second session we discussed our lists. I had had some trouble with mine. Rethinking past episodes had been difficult because I couldn't remember much. And when one of the counselors asked us to add to the list our feelings about Mom's behavior, I had even more difficulty. God had taken away my bitterness. I could say the words, but the anger and hurt behind them were gone.

When I explained my problem, the counselors didn't seem to believe me. Alcoholic family members often block out their feelings, so counselors are used to dealing with people who can't remember the pain. When I explained what Jesus did for me, however, they seemed satisfied with my answer.

Recent episodes were easier for me to relate than those from the distant past. God used the sessions to help me release much of the anger and frustration that had built up in recent months. The big box of Kleenex that was kept handy was empty by the end of the session.

During the following week I looked over my list and reflected on my true feelings. I recorded my fear and anxiety over Mom's blackouts. I remembered the embarrassment at restaurants and the looks on my children's faces when their grandmother stumbled down the stairs.

We worked on our lists for the next two sessions, until we had pinpointed the events and our feelings. The more evidence we presented, the more likely that Mom would begin to face reality. Writing, I found, was therapeutic. But there was a more important reason for putting everything on paper. If we got caught up in our emotions during the presentation, we would have something to refer to.

Finally we planned our meeting to confront Mom with our facts and feelings. Since most of our emotions had been expelled beforehand in our practice sessions, we could talk to her quietly and without accusations. The tone of our approach would be crucial to our success. And having the professionals on hand would insure that the conversations stayed on track. Alcoholics are known to try to sidestep the issues, and the counselors are trained to watch for such problems.

For our last assignment the counselors asked us to consider how we would react if Mom refused treatment again. This surprised me. Until now I had fended off doubts with positive thinking. Why prepare for the negative, I wondered.

For the next two weeks I tossed to and fro like a boat in a restless sea. My brothers decided to tell Mom they'd never see her again if she refused help. Could I say that and mean it? *Would* I say it? What did God want me to do?

Once again God used Scripture to answer me. I spent the entire week scouring the New Testament for everything Jesus said. Jesus was my example of love, and I knew He would show me the loving thing to do.

During my search, one passage stood out. "Take heed to yourself; if your brother sins, rebuke him, and if he repents, forgive him (Luke 17:3 RSV)." I believed God was telling me it was right for me to speak to my mother about her problems, using the same gentleness Jesus expressed, and that I needed to be prepared to offer her my forgiveness.

But what if Mom said no again? What should I do then?

I have learned that God sometimes uses circumstances and the advice of other Christians to speak to us in times of uncertainty. During this time of questioning, God used both. Just as I was wrestling over the assignment to write out my decision, God sent a stranger to my home.

This stranger was a woman who had recently started to attend our church. We had met briefly in the pastor's class the previous Sunday. As she sat down in my home, she explained that she needed to talk to someone and she felt that she could confide in me. She then poured out the story of her life prior to becoming a believer. She'd been into drugs, prostitution, and many other sinful activities. She had come back to Jesus, but now she was having a struggle to keep from falling back into her old ways.

I didn't realize why God had sent her to me until she explained how she had changed her ways. I was electrified as she began to tell the story of how her family finally confronted her. They forced her to choose between them and her sinful lifestyle. When I heard her words I realized it was no coincidence that she had arrived on my doorstep that day. God had sent her with a message, and He also gave me words of encouragement to share with her.

I knew then what I should do. I had to put my relationship with Mom on the line. I could no longer live with her problem. She would have to choose between me and the bottle.

But how could I say that convincingly to Mom? A few days later I came across 1 Samuel 16:6–7 in my daily Scripture reading. The Lord had sent Samuel to find a new king for Israel. When Samuel arrived he found Eliab and thought surely he must be the Lord's choice. But the Lord had someone else in mind and told Samuel: "Do not look on his appearance or on the height of his stature, because I have rejected him; for the Lord sees not as man sees; man looks on the outward appearance, but the Lord looks on the heart" RSV.

God had reminded me to look past my mother's outward appearance and examine her heart. He asked me to see Mom as He did. I needed to tell her as lovingly as possible what I saw.

After finishing my meditation, I wrote my final message to Mom. God gave me moving words of salvation and hope. I knew He could touch her if I would only have the courage to speak those words.

As we made the final preparations for our encounter, I was concerned about the education sessions we had missed. We had tried to arrange to see the other films privately, but no one could show them at a time we could attend. We had, however, read most of the books they recommended, and the counselors felt we were better prepared than most. I was still uneasy, though.

But I was in for one more little surprise. On the Sunday prior to our final session I received another unusual confirmation of our plans. Every Sunday before leaving for church, I try to watch Dr. Robert Schuller's *Hour of Power*. To my surprise, his guest speaker that morning was the author of one of the films we had missed in the education series! I absorbed every word he spoke. What he said confirmed what I already knew: In a loving manner confront the alcoholic with as much reality as possible. How wonderful of God to provide this additional comfort for me.

The key word I heard was "lovingly." How easy to condemn, how difficult to love. I reviewed all my statements one final time, checking to be sure my words were honest but without bitterness and anger. I felt a great love for Mom. I could only hope that she would feel it too.

The last few weeks of preparation were extremely difficult. The fifty-mile drive to the hospital was tiring, and I had to arrange for a babysitter for my three small children. And making the lists and reliving past hurts was physically and emotionally draining. I hated coming home with a puffy face, feeling tired, and having to face three energetic children and my husband. Only God's strength kept me going—and the support of my family and friends.

For our final meeting, everyone who would be involved in the intervention came together. We rehearsed our statements coupled with our feelings. The emotional tension reached a peak as my brothers shared things I'd never known. For the first time in our lives we were being honest with each other. I was glad Roger was able to join us for this last rehearsal. Sharing the experience with him provided the comfort I so desperately needed.

Miraculously, out of all that hurt came a new awareness of who we were. What a tremendous feeling. We had been through tough times, but now our relationship had a new solidarity. Could this be the gold that Peter talks about in 1 Peter 1:6–7? "In this you rejoice, though now for a little while you may have to suffer various trials, so that the genuineness of your faith, more precious than gold which though perishable is tested by fire, may redound to praise and glory and honor at the revelation of Jesus Christ" (RSV).

Finally we presented our closing statements, called "clout" statements. We would use them only if Mom said no. When I read mine, no one's eyes were dry. I couldn't keep back the tears myself. Printed on those pages were words I seriously hoped I would never have to say to my mother. Only the Holy Spirit could help me get through this.

We agreed on a date and time for the actual intervention. The counselors made sure a room was available at the hospital, and we finalized financial arrangements and discussed the actual commitment program. Mom would be admitted for thirty days. We could visit her often. She would receive three or four days of detoxification treatment and then be moved to a special ward where she would receive individual and group counseling. After she was discharged, the hospital would help her find a support group close to home. The aftercare program could last as long as two years.

I listened to the details, but I refused to expend my energy comtemplating all that they would involve. There would be time for that later, after we had successfully completed the planned encounter. Now I had to concentrate all my energy on how to get through that day.

7

Confrontation

Someone must want us to fail, I concluded when I awoke on the day we were scheduled to confront Mom. A raging snowstorm, only the second one we'd had all year, was clogging highways and had caused schools to close. We would have to take our children with us—assuming, of course, that we could get our car through the storm. Even that was beginning to look doubtful.

Up early because I could not sleep well, I turned to my daily devotional reading. "Simon, Simon, behold, Satan demanded to have you, that he might sift you like wheat, but I have prayed for you, that your faith might not fail" (Luke 22:31 RSV). Would I be tested this day, I wondered. Was this a warning?

I remembered another warning I'd received recently.

CONFRONTATION

Our church had promoted the film *Joni*, and it had prompted a discussion of some probing questions in our adult Bible class. At one time Joni had wondered whether her lack of faith was the reason she wasn't totally healed. But God showed her, over a period of time, that He had placed her in her circumstances and that she should trust Him.

Lack of faith was not going to get me down, I determined. Not today. I prayed for an increase in faith to get me through the day and asked for wisdom to decide if indeed we should proceed with the confrontation today.

The snowstorm didn't surprise me. I knew Satan would try to keep us from succeeding. But I was determined to get this next step accomplished. Too many details—the counselors' time schedule, the availability of a bed at the hospital, time off from work for everyone involved—had been worked out to abandon the plan now. We could lose the opportunity for good if we did. Besides, none of us knew how much longer we could hold up under the tension.

The biggest obstacle I faced, after deciding to proceed, was how to convince Mom to come along. We had debated about this in every session. My brothers felt I had a better chance than they of persuading her. The counselors suggested that we be as honest as possible, without spelling out all the details. As a last option, we could all go to Mom's house, but the counselors advised against that idea. Their experience had taught them that an alcoholic responds better in a neutral setting. It's too easy for alcoholics to become defensive in comfortable surroundings.

I had originally planned to invite Mom to take a drive in our new car, since she had not seen it yet. We would "happen" to end up at the hospital and, hopefully, I could then convince her to come inside and meet with us. I obviously had a problem with that solution. We couldn't "joy ride" in a snowstorm. How would I persuade Mom to even get into the car in this weather? Served me right for not being honest in the first place, I decided. Only a concentrated prayer effort would enable me to accomplish my purpose.

I had already called and written many friends and prayer groups and asked them to be in prayer at 9:30 that morning, the time we were scheduled to begin intervention. I asked them to pray that Mom would be open and would hear what we were saying to her.

Roger and I and the children left the house at 7:30 A.M., and spent the next hour and a half driving thirty miles in the blinding snowstorm. Despite the hazardous weather conditions, however, I felt no fear. God was in charge. We arrived at Mom's at the exact time I'd asked everyone to start praying.

We all popped in, and I explained to Mom that I needed to talk to her—with a counselor's help. She thought it would be ridiculous to go anywhere in such deplorable weather conditions and asked why we didn't postpone it for another day.

I pleaded with her and explained how important this was to me. I promised that I would never ask her to go to a counselor again if she would just hear me out today. All our prayers were answered. Mom reluctantly agreed to come along.

Traveling was hazardous. We spun out once and arrived at the hospital an hour and a half late because we had to drive so slowly. I hoped the others had not given up and left. Since we had realized ahead of time that I could not call from Mom's if I saw we were going to be late, we had arranged for one of my brothers to call her house if we had not arrived at the hospital by 10 A.M. I hoped the plan had worked. It had. They were waiting when we arrived. They had tried calling and, when no one answered, realized we had left.

I helped the children get settled in an outer area, then joined the others. Mom didn't seem surprised to see my brothers there. The counselors introduced themselves, offered us coffee, and helped us get seated in the circle of chairs. They explained to Mom that we had some important feelings to share with her and asked that she listen, without commenting, to everything we had to say. She would have a chance to answer us when we were finished. From experience, the counselors knew that alcoholics become defensive when confronted with the facts of their behavior. They try to sidetrack the issue by interrupting and flinging out accusations. The most effective way to reach them is to continually hit them with facts until they are forced to see the truth. So when Mom agreed to these conditions we all breathed a sigh of relief.

Trembling and nervous, we began the confrontation. My youngest brother was first. He had to stop several times to gain control of his emotions. Then came my turn.

"Mom," I began, "I came here today because I am deeply concerned about what's been happening to you. Your drinking seriously affects me *and* my family. What I have to say will be painful, but I'd like to ask you to hear me out.

"I don't think you realize how I feel when I see you drinking again. It takes me back to the times when, as a youngster, I saw you drinking. Very often, drinking made you unreasonable. For example, I remember signing up as a school guard in the sixth grade. I needed your permission. When I came home you were drinking. You flew into a rage and said no, you wanted me home. Having to go back and say I couldn't do it was humiliating. And more embarrassing, I didn't have a reason. I felt so angry—and I felt afraid. I never knew how you would react to any request I made.

"There were days when I wanted to invite my friends in or when I wanted to go out, but I couldn't. You continually threw up after drinking, and I had to clean up the messes. I had to do most of the housework, too. I resented that. I felt cheated out of a normal life.

"As your drinking got worse, most of the money we had went to buy bottles. When a bottle broke once, and I cut my knee badly, I couldn't get the help I needed and I felt so scared. I also remember not telling anyone when I was hit by a car because I was afraid. I had hurt my arm, but you weren't able to get up and get help for me. When one of my teachers sent me to the nurse the following day, she asked me why I hadn't seen a doctor. I felt too ashamed to admit that you had been drinking and couldn't take me, so I lied instead and said you were sick. I felt angry that I had to lie for you.

"Finally I became anxious and worried about what was happening to you. My school work began to suffer. I cried a lot, but I refused to tell anyone at school why. I was terrified that if they knew the truth they would take us away from you.

"Then you stopped drinking. We never talked about that, but in many ways it made such a difference in my life. You were able to do housekeeping chores again, and

I felt free to develop friends and a life of my own for the first time. But because I felt a wall between us, I couldn't share my important feelings with you, and that hurt.

"The years went by, and then something happened. Aunt Maybelle died in February 1977, four years ago. You appeared to take it well, but you refused to talk about your feelings. I needed to talk, but you refused and hung up when I called. That hurt me very much. Then things began to change. I noticed that your letters, which usually came twice a month, stopped coming. I had enjoyed receiving them, and I felt shut out of your life. That hurt too, and I began to feel anxious about you.

"You came to visit us in May of that year. When we went out for dinner you ordered a drink. I felt a pit of fear opening up in my stomach. I had not seen you take a drink since I was sixteen. I watched your behavior change from calm to giggly and weaving, and I wanted to throw up. I tried to pretend nothing was wrong.

"In the winter of 1978 you fell and broke your arm. We were visiting you at the time. I had heard from Bruce and Richard that you were drinking again. Because I loved you, I wanted to believe that you fell on the ice, sober, but I was so distrustful and confused. I didn't know who to believe. I was in Chicago the next week and tried calling to check on how you were doing. I couldn't get an answer for three days. I was so frantic I called your employer. Your boss told me you hadn't shown up for work either and that he had given you a warning slip because it wasn't the first time it had happened. I was shocked.

"We met with you shortly after that to try to convince you to seek help. We all went to see a crisis counselor and, for the first time, you shared your real feelings about some things. It hurt me to hear you out, but I felt relief, too. We had made a beginning. And I was elated when you agreed to go with Richard to De Paul for counseling.

"But when you then refused to go on with the counseling I felt so helpless. Up to that point I still had not seen you drinking regularly, so I rationalized that things weren't so bad.

"Then I came to pick you up that summer for your checkup. I had the girls with me and we were going out to lunch together. You weaved down the stairs and refused to unlock the door and let us in. You had been drinking. When Amy asked, 'What's the matter with Grandma, Mommy, she's acting funny?' I was embarrassed and angry. I felt like slapping you, and that horrified me. I loved you, but you were hurting me and my family. I was so frustrated.

"My inner frustration grew so much worse that my physical health began to suffer. My skin allergies became so violent that I could no longer cope. I knew that somehow this situation had to be resolved. So Roger found a job up here, and we moved.

"Just after we arrived, you had another fall. This time you broke your back and your foot. I knew you had been drinking and had blacked out. When I went into your house a week later and saw the bloodstains on the floor I was sick to my stomach. And I hurt inside, thinking that it could have been worse. When I went upstairs you were throwing up. I felt sorry for you and angry with myself. It was as if the clock had rolled back and nothing had ever changed.

"A few weeks later I decided to see a counselor. I stopped by your house unexpectedly to ask you to go with me. We sat down in the living room and talked about everyday things. Inside I felt like screaming. Suddenly I noticed that you were sitting on a bottle. A moment later I noticed another one in a bag next to the couch. I felt like crying. You looked so pathetic sitting on that bottle, and I felt so helpless trying to talk to you.

"In December when we were downtown I finally realized how much your health had been affected by your drinking. You could barely walk, you were winded, and you couldn't climb up the curb without help. I suddenly saw you as a really old person, and I felt sorry for you.

"And now you've lost your job. Your boss called me to explain. He revealed that on four separate occasions this year you had to be taken home because you had been drinking and couldn't perform your duties as a nurse. I felt so ashamed.

"Mom, when you drink you become a different person. I am frightened by your mood changes. You laugh at things that aren't funny and you repeat yourself. You get angry with me, and then a day or two later you can't even remember that we talked.

"On the other hand, there is such a difference when you're sober. I enjoyed going downtown with you and the girls for breakfast. And the girls were so happy to share a treat with Grandma. What a joyful experience it was to attend church together on Christmas Eve. And having you with us on Christmas turned into a special occasion—because you had not been drinking. Alcohol makes such a difference.

"Other people notice the difference too. Your boss made a point of telling me that you'd be missed at work. He also told me that he wrote on your report that he would recommend rehiring you *if* you would enroll in a rehabilitation program. He thinks there's hope for you. "I think there's hope for you too. Because I love you, I'm asking you to get help today, before it's too late."

I had made it through my recitation—but barely. I reached for the box of Kleenex to dry my face and eyes as my brother began to share his list. He appeared to be the calmest, but his voice belied his calm expression. He read his list quietly and ended with the same appeal the rest of us used.

The counselors briefly explained to Mom the rehabilitation program we were suggesting and told how it could help her. We couldn't tell from her expression how she was reacting. She had refused to take off her coat, and she looked as if she would fly out of the room at any moment. Once she smoked a cigarette. Occasionally she brushed away a tear. Nothing else gave us a clue as to what she was feeling when we shared with her what we saw happening.

I held my breath when the counselors finally asked Mom for her response. I expected a rebuttal, arguments, defensive statements, accusations. I braced myself for the attack, but I was not prepared for Mom's answer.

Quietly and calmly she told us her decision. A simple "No" was all she said.

8

Clout

Now what were we going to do? I had expected a long, angry tirade, not this. The counselors, however, suspected this might happen and so they had had us prepare a "clout" statement. We had one more opportunity to get our point across.

The counselors explained to Mom that because of her answer we had some other important feelings to share with her. We followed the same order of sharing.

My brothers simply stated that if she refused help they wanted nothing more to do with her. They would be more than happy, however, to work with her through a rehabilitation program if she agreed to get help. They emphasized to her that either she wanted a productive life again or she wanted the bottle; she couldn't have both.

My approach was slightly different from theirs.

"Mom," I began, "you know I have a tremendous faith in God. From the very beginning I've believed that somehow the problem with your drinking was going to work out. I encouraged my brothers to hang on through the darkest hours because I believed that we could get through to you.

"I know that my human nature turned many of my feelings to anger and hatred. I felt I had a right to those feelings. It wasn't until I met God and came to know His forgiving love that I could begin to understand what love really is. Sometimes that meant putting on God's eyeglasses and looking through the outside of a person to see what was inside the person's heart.

"The reason I could offer encouragement to my brothers through all this was because I looked at you with God's glasses and saw inside to the person God created you to be. I knew that underneath your hard exterior was a kernel of a beautiful person. With the proper help and much understanding that kernel could break out.

"It would break my heart if you refused help today. But I also know that loving someone also means letting go. I never thought I would reach the point of letting you go. But as I read my Bible and prayed in recent weeks and asked God to help me know what to do, He showed me the answer in His Word.

Proverbs 23:29–35 says, "Who has woe? Who has sorrow? Who has strife? Who has complaints? Who has needless bruises? Who has bloodshot eyes? Those who linger over wine, who go to sample bowls of mixed wine. Do not gaze at wine when it is red, when it sparkles in the cup, when it goes down smoothly! In the end it bites like a snake and poisons like a viper. Your eyes will see strange sights and your mind imagine confusing things. You will be like one sleeping on the high seas, lying on top of the rigging. 'They hit me,' you will say, 'but I'm not hurt! They beat me, but I don't feel it! When will I wake up so I can find another drink?' "

"God gives every person a chance to make a choice. Now you must choose. If you refuse help today you are as good as dead. You cannot keep drinking without killing yourself. And if you don't get help today I'm walking out this door and I'll have nothing more to do with you. As much as it would hurt me to walk out of your life, it would hurt me more to stand by and watch you die.

"I moved up here with my family to work together with you and my brothers to build the family God wants us to be. I desperately want to have you with us. There is only one thing that stands between us—a bottle. You have to choose what's more important to you—the bottle or your family. I'm hoping and praying that you'll choose us."

The tears were streaming down my face as I read the words. I looked once more at my mother's face, silently pleading with her to listen to me. But once again she simply looked at us and softly answered, "No."

Anger welled up inside me and I was grateful for the presence of the counselors. They asked us all to sit quietly for a few minutes and think through what had been said. After a moment or two I became aware that everyone in the room was watching for my reactions. For the last four years I had been positive that God would grant my request and that I would see my mother cured. Whenever I heard my brothers expressing doubts I encouraged them with Scripture. My God wouldn't fail; yet apparently He had.

I reflected on the misery of the past four years. I thought about all the pain we'd endured, the humiliation, and the embarrassment. I had managed to hold on through it all because I earnestly believed that in the end we would succeed.

Now I had to live up to the brave words I'd spoken. I had told Mom I'd walk out and never see her again. I believed it was the right thing to do. I silently pleaded with God to send me a word of encouragement, something to sustain me, for I needed Him now more than ever. Suddenly the Scripture verse I had read earlier that morning flooded back into my mind. "Simon, Simon [Janet, Janet], behold, Satan demanded to have you, that he might sift you like wheat, but I have prayed for you, that your faith might not fail."

I felt electrified. Was *my* faith being tested here? How was I going to react to my mother's decision? Would I obey God and walk out as I felt He told me to do? Or would I fall into Satan's trap?

God knew what He was doing. He had built a foundation of faithfulness in me all these years. I'd never had a reason to doubt Him before, and I didn't have one now. I felt the comfort of His loving arms surround me in that room, and I knew that everything would be all right. Even though I couldn't understand all that was happening, someday I would. It was enough for me to know that God was still in charge.

More calmly, then, I questioned Mom a little longer. I asked her if she realized how empty her life would be without a family. She said she understood. Her life was her own, she added, and she would live it the way she chose.

The counselors gave Mom their card, in case she ever

decided she needed help, and asked her to wait outside for a few minutes. I could hear my children greet Mom as she left the room. Then the door closed behind her. It was over. We had lost.

The counselors, concerned about our reactions, turned their attention toward us. Mom was much sicker than anyone realized, they explained, assuring us that we had done everything possible to reach her and that we were not to blame for her answer. They urged us to consider attending their family after-care program as a way of taking care of ourselves. I wrote down the telephone number for the program and promised to call for information. I was too numb to say anything more. As we got up to leave, however, I realized it really was over. I broke down. I had just watched my hopes get crushed, and it hurt.

I received the comforting hugs of the people I loved, knowing that they too were hurting. With nothing left to say, we opened the door and went out.

Roger agreed to drive Mom home. Knowing that I'd probably never see her again, I couldn't face saying good-bye to her at her house. The children and I would go back with my brothers. I told my children to hug Grandma and say good-bye for the last time, hoping that this little drama would make an impression on her.

Roger told me later that some of what we had said must have gotten through to her. As they drove home Mom angrily told him that she didn't believe most of the things we had said. She refused to take responsibility for what had happened.

Before dropping her off, Roger drove through a cemetery and pointed out to Mom that this was where she would end up if she didn't stop drinking. He asked her to do some serious thinking. Then he prayed over her and asked God to keep her in His care.

And so we left. A part of my life was over. I could only pray that God would give me the strength to put it all behind me and would help me move ahead.

9

Discovering Why We Failed

I cried all the way home. In spite of the blessed assurance God gave me, I remained depressed and upset. I staged a mini-rebellion against God during the next few weeks by refusing to study the Scriptures. I was angry at God for making a fool of me, and I didn't want to hear what He had to say. I felt justified in clinging to my hurt.

The family after-care treatment kept coming to mind, so I called for information. They met two days a week for a month to explore feelings and discuss new directions for our lives. I was unable to get excited about going. I would have to drive a long distance, the program was costly, and I would have to find and pay a sitter for my children. And I wasn't even sure if they could provide the spiritual direction I so desperately needed.

I knew God had a lesson for me in this defeat, but I wasn't ready to hear His answers—at least not yet.

I decided the best therapy would be to get out of the house and stop sitting around and brooding. I applied for a job at a local company that had an opening suited to my abilities and went home to await their decision. After three additional interviews, the company still was unable to decide. The more time they took, the more I began thinking about what commitments God wanted me to make. As the anger and hurt subsided, I realized a desperate need for some answers from God. I was finally ready to be taught.

When I am ready to listen, God speaks loudly and clearly. As soon as I opened my Bible I read, "Do not lose heart. Though our outer nature is wasting away, our inner nature is being renewed every day. For this slight momentary affliction is preparing us for an eternal weight of glory beyond all comparison, because we do not look to the things that are seen but to the things that are unseen" (2 Corinthians 4:16–18 RSV).

I understood some of what God was saying: Don't lose heart. I had experienced a "momentary affliction," but God encouraged me to look past the present hurt to the future glory. I couldn't see what was coming, but God knew, and He asked me to trust Him further. The Lord knew exactly what I needed to hear.

Then I read Romans 8:35–37: "Who can separate us from the love of God? Shall tribulation, or distress, or persecution, or famine, or nakedness, or peril, or sword? . . . No, in all these things we are more than conquerors through him who loved us" (RSV).

To me that meant that not one single thing—physical hurts, loss of job, temptation, emotional hurts—could block out God's love unless I allowed it to. Would I let my experiences destroy me, or would I choose to overcome them? Would I let this defeat stand between me and His love? No. I would gladly give up anything—even my mother—if it meant keeping God's love.

What sweet victory Jesus gives when we allow Him to walk us through the valleys. "Yea, though I walk through the valley of the shadow of death, I will fear no evil: for thou art with me . . . "(Psalm 23:4 KJV).

I finally began to accept *what* had happened, but I still had to know *why* it had happened. I had prayed, prepared, and spoken in love. Yet still I failed. Had God decided to punish me for some sin I was unaware of?

When I turned to Scripture for an answer, the words of the Lord came through clearly. In Luke 16 I read the account of a rich man who died and went to Hell and Lazarus, a beggar who died and "was carried to Abraham's bosom." Looking up from Hell, the rich man asked that the poor man be allowed to give him some water, but his request was denied because of the great gulf between them. The rich man then asked Abraham to send Lazarus to warn his brothers to repent. But this request also was denied. "If they do not hear Moses and the prophets, neither will they be convinced if someone should rise from the dead," Abraham replied (v. 31 RSV).

My mother, this passage helped me realize, was the one who had the choice to make, not I. I had prayed that she would hear what we said and choose God. She had indeed heard what we said, so my prayers were answered, and she made her choice, even though it was not the one God and I wanted her to make. If the circumstances, our words, or the timing had been changed, it would have made no difference. As the verse says, even sending someone from the dead would not help. My mother hardened her heart by her own choice. Now I had to let go of her and relinquish her care to God.

What a beautiful moment of release I experienced then. I realized the truth of what I'd just read. No matter how much I wanted my mother to be saved, she had to want it for herself. And no matter how much God wants us to follow His way, He won't force Himself on us if we refuse Him. He leaves the choice to us. I found comfort in knowing that God shared the same frustration I felt.

I realized that for the past few weeks I had been plagued by doubts—doubts that I could now confess as sin. I had done what I believed was right, and now I had to go on from there. I still had some questions, though, so I prayed that God would provide answers through His Word.

As I began to search the Gospels, I set up two conditions for my study. First, I would note only those Scriptures in which Jesus said something pertaining to my questions. Second, I would write down all verses, negative or positive, that had any bearing on the subject. Studying the Scripture in this manner gave me a new understanding of myself and new insights into my situation. After reading Matthew 10:37 I realized that I had allowed my love for my mother to become something more than it should have been. Mom and I had always had a reversed relationship, which wasn't right. When I chose to walk away from her, God broke those unhealthy bonds.

Matthew 13:57 encouraged me that even Jesus was "without honor in his own country." Because He was so familiar to his neighbors (after all, everyone knew his brothers and sisters and parents), they could not see how extraordinary He really was. Similarly, because the people closest to us know us best, they are the most difficult people to witness to. That does not mean, of course, that we shouldn't witness to them—only that the job is more difficult.

"I have not come to call the righteous, but sinners to repentance," Jesus said in Luke 5:32. My mother needed to hear that call to repentance, and I believed God used me to relate it. I was not, however, responsible for her response to the call.

My conviction that Mom had made her own choice was reinforced by reading Matthew 22:14: "For many are called, but few are chosen." God speaks to many, but not everyone answers. Mom had been invited to put her faith in Christ; she chose not to. Not everyone wants to be a soldier in God's army.

I was reminded of the contrast between my mother and me when I read Matthew 25:29: "For to everyone who has will more be given, and he will have abundance; but from him who has not, even what he has will be taken away." I had so much to be thankful for. My mother, on the other hand, had nothing left. I knew God would supply my needs out of His abundance; my mother had no such assurance, no one to supply her needs.

These were just a few of the verses that gave me a better understanding of how God was working in my life. Other passages, however, caused me to ask even more questions.

Matthew 5:46 made me wonder if it was really love or perhaps only selfish desire that made me walk away from my mother. "For if you love those who love you, what reward have you? Do not even the tax collectors do the same?" the verse asked. My mother didn't make it easy for me to love her, but didn't she need my love more than ever now that she was down and out?

I wrestled with this question only to be confronted by another that had popped up before: Who was I to tell Mom how to live? Wasn't I judging her by my standards? The warning in Luke 6:37 caught my attention. "Judge not, and you will not be judged; condemn not, and you will not be condemned; forgive, and you will be forgiven." I knew how easily one could fall into temptation. I personally struggle with being overweight and find it impossible at times to control my appetite. Am I any better than Mom? Is her alcoholism any worse than my overeating? What right do I have to point a finger at her?

The conflict was clear, and I was becoming confused. I forced myself to look at the cold facts: My mother would die without help. I could not stand by in cowardly silence. Somewhere in all of this there had to be a formula for compromise.

Two important phone calls came while I was muddling my way through all this. From the first call I learned that I had lost the job I'd been waiting for. That hurt, but I wasn't surprised. I suspected that God had something else He wanted me to do. Just after I hung up, the phone rang again. One of the intervention counselors and some colleagues, in discussing our case, had come up with another alternative—legal commitment. He gave me some numbers to call if I wanted more information.

Just when I had begun to accept my loss I was faced with another dilemma. Did this mean that our previous loss was just one battle and that God was giving us another opportunity? Or was this a temptation to get me on the merry-go-round again? How was I to know?

I went into prayer and emerged with another fleece-lined decision. I couldn't deny any opportunity to help Mom. I knew, however, that legal commitment required the cooperation of three people, so I couldn't do this alone. I would leave the decision in my brothers' hands. I wrote them both a simple letter, stating the facts as I had learned them. I said nothing to coerce them or influence their decision. If they were willing, we'd do it; if either one said no, the deal was off.

As I mailed the letters, I wondered what their replies would be and where this action would take us. In my heart, though, I knew it didn't matter either way. I had already crossed the bridge of trust with God. He didn't have to prove anything any more.

10

Legal Commitment

Legal commitment is a very serious step to consider taking. It carries some risks. The law generally supports the person being committed. There is no guarantee you will win if you try to have someone committed, and often you're not really even sure you want to win.

Financially, the proceedings may be a burden. Emotionally, working things out in a courtroom may be too much to face. Legal commitment is absolutely the last resort, and usually only desperate people use it.

Requirements for legal commitment vary from state to state and, in my state, they actually vary from county to county. The intervention counselors worked in a different county than the one in which either my mother or I lived, and so the facts they gave me proved to be wrong.

LEGAL COMMITMENT

The requirements for legal commitment in my county were much more stringent than those that had been explained to me. The only way we could have Mom committed in our county was if she lived with us. Since we weren't even seeing Mom, that would be an unlikely arrangement.

I called the officials in the county where my mother lived, and a helpful clerk explained the basic procedure. Three people would have to come to the courthouse and testify that within the past six months, because of alcoholism, the individual had suffered physical harm, lost the ability to be financially self-supporting, been a potential danger to others, and suffered falls or blackouts. After documents with this information were typed and taken to the county prosecutor's office, the alcoholic would be picked up, hospitalized, and scheduled for a court appearance. Those who had provided the initial testimony would be asked to swear in court that their statements were true and to answer additional questions. After talking to the alcoholic, the judge would make a decision. If the judge decided treatment was in order, the alcoholic would be sent to the county hospital so the court could monitor his or her progress. The family had no choice as to treatment centers.

I dreaded the thought of going through this all over again. My life had just begun to return to a more normal state. Emotionally, I was beginning to feel healthy, and I wasn't sure I wanted to destroy my peace of mind. But Mom was a very sick woman, and getting her off alcohol was the only way to prolong her life. I loved her and wanted to see her well. So much to be gained; so little to lose. I knew God would give me the strength to face this one more time.

Perhaps now the timing was better. Mom had had time to think about what we'd said. I became more and more hopeful as I anxiously awaited my brothers' responses.

Finally they both called and agreed that we should try this last avenue of hope. I arranged an appointment for us with the county clerk, who would take our depositions, and we met several days later at the courthouse steps and walked in together.

I was surprised at how many emotions were triggered by this visit. My parents had received their divorce in this courthouse; and we were involved in several custody battles in one of its rooms. There seemed to be no way to escape the many painful memories of the past.

We managed to find the clerk's office, a tiny cubicle with barely enough room for everyone to squeeze into. The clerk was patient and kind as he briefly reiterated the procedure and answered our questions. We were alarmed to learn, however, some facts we had not been aware of. First, these procedures would end in our swearing out a warrant for Mom's arrest. After the papers were processed, she would be arrested and taken to the hospital for detoxification. I shuddered at such a chilling thought. I had not pictured anyone actually taking Mom away from her home.

Second, no matter how good our case seemed, the law supported Mom's rights. As an individual, she was free to do what she wanted to do. The burden of proof was on us.

The clerk also explained that a lawyer would be appointed for Mom if she couldn't afford one. The thought of my mother having to hire a lawyer to work against her family appalled me. We had only her best interests at heart. All we wanted was a reunion with her.

LEGAL COMMITMENT 83

The clerk added, however, that often a lawyer will encourage the client to make a voluntary commitment rather than fight it out in court. There was a chance then that we might be spared a courtroom scene if things went well.

What caused me the most doubts about the procedure was learning that a judge could only commit Mom legally for thirty days. After that the alcoholic would either accept rehabilitation or return to the bottle. If Mom refused to accept help at the end of thirty days, we would have to repeat the court action. Suppose Mom stubbornly refused to cooperate. We knew that was a possibility. Would we, could we, go through this over and over? I knew I couldn't. I had tasted a few months of peaceful freedom. I didn't want to be locked up in this mess again. I reasoned, however, that I owed this process at least one try. Any glimmer of hope was worth whatever I'd have to go through. I decided to proceed.

We spent the next three hours identifying dates and times of incidents that proved our mother desperately needed help. The lists we had prepared for the intervention were serving another useful purpose. The clerk seemed surprised that we were so well-prepared.

We ate lunch while the formal statements were being typed. When we returned later that afternoon, we signed the depositions, had them notarized, and took them upstairs to the prosecutor's office. While waiting in the pleasant reception area, I began to feel nervous as well-dressed men, seemingly on important business, came and went.

Finally an administrative assistant came to take our documents. She returned a few minutes later to ask us some questions about the impending arrest. "Was mother likely to cooperate when the officers arrived?" she asked.

When we answered no, she noted that handcuffs might be necessary. Then she asked if Mom would open the door for an officer. When we answered no again, she said that one of us would have to be present to admit the officer to the premises. Both my brothers shook their head no, indicating that the responsibility would be left to me.

I pictured my mother being taken away, and I thought of Judas watching Jesus being taken away after the betrayal. Could I stand there and watch such a scene? I agonized in prayer. What was happening here? I loved my mother and only wanted to help her? How, in God's name, had we come to this?

But then I slowly remembered that we had tried every reasonable way to help Mom. Her stubborn refusals led us to this desperate act. She had brought this upon herself. I thought of the courage it had taken to get this far, and I knew I would find the courage to face this problem too with God's help.

Finally I agreed to be there. I gave the woman my phone number so she could call me when a time was arranged. She thought it might take three or four days. We still had to speak with the prosecuting attorney, so his assistant asked us to step into his office.

"I notice that the last date of your allegations was February 10, two months ago," the attorney said after quietly reviewing our statements. "When was the last time you saw your mother?"

We briefly explained what had happened at the intervention and why we had not seen Mom since.

"I'm sorry," he told us gently. "Even though you have

more than enough evidence here, since you haven't seen your mother lately I can't have her picked up. There is a slim chance that she may have received treatment during the last couple months. We can't risk the embarrassment of arresting her without cause. However, if one of you would go see her today and come back with an updated report of her condition, our case would be tight. As it is now, though, the judge would throw it out on that one technicality."

I was stunned. I couldn't believe what I was hearing. I felt as if someone had slammed a door in my face. To come this close only to be defeated again ... I knew at that very moment that it was all over. God had made the message very clear to me. "Let go," He said, and He meant it.

No one spoke for a moment, then I thanked the prosecutor for his time and told him we'd get back to him. Quietly and unhurriedly we walked out of the offices, down the hall, and took the stairs to the main door. As I walked out into the sunshine I felt my self-control slipping. Shivering in spite of the warm sunshine, I stopped and turned to my brothers. I searched their faces for some sign to match the turbulent emotion I felt. None was there. Defeated again. I wanted to scream. We came so close only to have victory snatched away. Why?

"We could simply lie and say we had gone to see her," I said wistfully. But I knew I could never do that. "We could go back and see Mom just once more ... " but the words died. I knew and they knew that we couldn't go back. Maybe it was pride, maybe it was part of being realistic, but there wasn't any point in going back any more.

I cried out to God from those courthouse steps. "Forgive me, Lord. I'm getting out of the way by stepping aside. It's over. She belongs to you now. Take care of her for us." With tears streaming down my face, I linked arms with my brothers and we walked away.

I had tried my best—and lost—but I had a beautiful family waiting at home for me, and it was time for them to receive my attention. Mom had taken four years of my life and kept them in constant turmoil. It was time to let the past die, once and for all, and look ahead to the future. For too long I had been tied up—physically, emotionally, and spiritually—with a problem that wasn't my own. There on those steps, God granted me freedom. I was going home a better person, and without the bitterness and anger I'd felt toward God before. I knew He loved me; He had satisfied my lingering doubts about His answers. Even though Mom refused my love and help, others would be open and willing to receive it. My job wasn't over—it was just beginning. God had more work to be done for His kingdom. I was finally free to do it.

11

What's Left to Say?

I thought a long time about committing to paper the lessons God taught me. At times I wondered if I had the right to speak on this subject. At other times I felt obligated to do so. Deciding to share such a personal experience, however, was not easy. But if only one person learns something from what I've written, then I will feel the task worthwhile.

I cannot say that everyone who faces the problem of alcoholism should follow the steps I've taken. I can say, however, that God has a plan for anyone who desires to walk in His footsteps. The first decision everyone must make, therefore, must be to seek out His plan. We have to want to know God's answers. The Bible says, "Therefore, do not be anxious, saying 'What shall we eat?' or 'What shall we wear?' ... but seek first His kingdom and his righteousness, and all these things shall be yours as well" (Matthew 6:31–33 RSV). If we first seek God's wisdom, He will answer.

I'm not a biblical scholar. I'm simply someone who tries to spend time each day studying God's Word and tries to put His truths to practice as much as I can. I recorded here what I learned. You must decide for yourself what the truth is, and then apply it to your situation.

I feel, however, that there are some basic principles that must be stated. First, although alcoholism has many of the symptoms of an illness, it is also a sin. The Scriptures I quoted in the introduction have convinced me of this. "The Devil's chloroform is the denial of sin," wrote Dennis DeHaan in *Our Daily Bread*.[1] This, I believe, is one reason it is sometimes so difficult to get through to alcoholics. They have hidden the facts from themselves and built up a denial system to avoid facing the reality of their sin. And they try to convince others to deny it too. In reality, acknowledgment of sin, whether people call it that or not, is the first step to recovery.

This is one reason I am convinced believers should be very cautious about working through secular counseling programs. Many non-Christian counselors cannot understand or do not accept the concept of sin. I found that it was best to take what was good from these programs and disclaim what did not follow God's truth.

Second, I am convinced that living in an alcoholic home produced family behaviors that were also an illness. I built a wall of protection around myself to keep the hurt out. Eventually that wall almost destroyed me. This illness, though, is also a sin, I believe. God did not create us to live that way. He wants us to be open and honest with one another.

In the end, the love of Jesus Christ broke the barrier of my defenses. Through the indwelling of the Holy Spirit, I learned to rebuild my life by exposing the hurts to God's healing love. And through the loving support of Christians in prayer groups and good, solid teaching and Bible study, God replaced my anger and bitterness with love. The process has worked for seventeen years, and I have no reason to doubt that it will continue for the rest of my life.

As part of the rebuilding process, I learned to face the ugly truth and deal with it. I faced the embarrassments, I faced the questions, and I pursued the answers because I knew God was in control and that He would carry me through each experience. As I encountered trying circumstances, I wrestled with deeper truths. I felt a responsibility to speak to my mother about her problem, but I had to examine myself closely to be certain that I spoke from love and not from judgment. Looking back, I see the simple reality of the situation: Even though I was careful to be loving and not judgmental in my confrontation, I could not change someone who refused to accept the truth. I could choose to become bitter about it, which would only destroy my peace, or I could choose to turn the matter over to God and let Him deal with it. I finally chose the latter.

"People with the best chance of sustaining well-being, then, are those willing to let go," wrote Gail Sheehy in *Pathfinders*.[2] For me, letting go of my mother was like watching my child walk for the first time. Falls, hurts, and bruises are inevitable, but learning to walk alone is a critical stage of development. Whether the experience will be tragic or delightful is something we won't know until they've tried it on their own.

After "letting Mom go," though, I learned there was a delicate balance between looking after myself and looking after others. Either extreme is harmful, and I had to be careful not to go from one to the other—from being overly concerned about Mom to being overly concerned about myself.

I leave this experience with a mixture of feelings. Most of them are good. A few are painful. But the blessings I've received overshadow the pain. My brothers and I have grown much closer through this experience. We behave more like a real family now. I've learned the value of dealing honestly with my feelings. I've also learned to temper that honesty with love and concern for others.

Above all, I know the peace that passes all understanding. I no longer worry about what will happen to Mom. I used to be afraid she'd start a fire while smoking in bed, or fall and be left helpless. Now I am confident that God is in charge. When He wants me to do something, He'll let me know.

I have not actually seen Mom since the intervention, but God has kept me in touch with her. Last summer a cousin I hadn't seen in twenty years called to tell me he had dropped by to visit Mom. She didn't look well, he said, and he wondered if she was sick, so he called me to find out. I knew his call wasn't a coincidence. Since then I've received two calls from strangers who had also spoken to Mom and wondered if she was sick. Even though the news about my mother gives little reason for optimism, I am thankful that God is keeping me informed about her condition.

For me, the final chapter isn't closed yet. My mother

knows I am just a phone call away. I told her when we parted that I would always love her, and I will. I continue to surround her with prayer, and I ask others to do likewise.

To those of you who are struggling over what to do about an alcoholic loved one, I offer this advice: Speak out in love. Honestly review your situation. Is silence worth the price you have to pay for it? If you add up the cost and find that it's not, get busy finding out how you can reach out and help your alcoholic recover. Please don't wait until it's too late.

For those of you who may have a drinking problem of your own and perhaps are reading this only because you promised a friend or relative that you would, I have only one suggestion: Please read carefully the words I have written. You have a family who loves you and wants you restored to them. Look at their faces and search their hearts. See the love shining there. Listen to what they are saying, and try to hear what they aren't. Reach out and receive—before it's too late.

I have learned how good family life can be. I've seen good family models, and Roger and I have tried to make ours one as well. The possibilities are endless when the foundation is honesty and trust. Don't settle for less than the best.

Having learned a lot from this experience, both about God and about myself, I have gone on with my life in a way that I believe is pleasing to the Lord. And I will continue to try.

" . . . so that we may no longer be children, tossed to and fro and carried about with every wind of doctrine, by the cunning of men, by their craftiness in deceitful wiles. Rather, speaking the truth in love, we are to grow up in every way into him who is the head, into Christ ... " (Eph. 4:14–15).

God bless your search.

Epilogue

Just prior to the publication of this book, I received word that my mother had reached another crisis and needed help. Faced with a predicament she could not solve and that threatened her independent lifestyle, she finally realized what her drinking had done to herself and to her family. She agreed to go into treatment and to accept the help we had lovingly offered so many times before.

We praise God for this recent development and for his sovereignty in each aspect of this experience.

Notes

Introduction

[1] Composite of notes taken from Family Education Series, Elmbrook Memorial Hospital, Brookfield, Wisconsin.

[2] Marmor, John, "Children of Alcoholics Get a Helping Hand," *Los Angeles Times*, (December 4, 1980), 1.

[3] Erdmann, Jake, "Statistics on Alcoholism Are Serious," *Westine Report*, (January 14, 1982), 11.

Chapter 2

[1] Luther, Martin, *Luther's Small Catechism*, (St. Louis: Concordia Publishing House, 1943), 64.

Chapter 5

[1] Sheehy, Gail, *Pathfinders*, (New York: William Morrow Co., 1982), Chapter 12, "Faith."

[2]"This is Al-Anon," (New York: Al-Anon Family Group Headquarters, 1967), 3–4.

[3]Alcoholics Victorious, National Headquarters, 123 S. Green Street, Chicago, IL 60607. (Write to this address for a list of active chapters.)

[4]Johnson, Vernon, *I'll Quit Tomorrow*, (New York: Harper and Row, 1973).

Chapter 6

[1]Johnson, Vernon, *I'll Quit Tomorrow*, (New York: Harper and Row, 1973), 49–51.

Chapter 11

[1]DeHaan, Dennis, ed., *Our Daily Bread*, (Grand Rapids: Radio Bible Class).

[2]Sheehy, Gail, *Pathfinders*, (New York: William Morrow Co., 1982), 60.